Blue Ribbon Conventions on BridgeBee

Scan this QR code with your smart phone to go directly to Randy Baron's Two Over One **BridgeBee** set.

How to scan a QR code: Open the Camera app on your phone, and point your phone at the QR code to scan it. Then tap the pop-up notification that appears at the top of your screen.

BridgeBee is the best new interactive way to play bridge and improve your game. The website is simple and intuitive to use.

With **BridgeBee** you won't form bad habits - if you select the wrong bid or card, you just try again until you get it right. Comments from experts and teachers will guide you through the lesson every step of the way.

Visit **www.BridgeBee.app** to learn more.

Randy Baron founded Baron Barclay Bridge Supplies in 1974 with his wife Mary, and was president of the company for over 30 years. He is well-known in the bridge world as a teacher, author, columnist, and expert. He has edited and published more than 200 books at Baron Barclay. Randy's many books and teaching materials include ABTA Book of the Year, the Bridge Book Series, written with Frank Stewart. His latest books are *Almost the Only Bridge Book You Will Ever Need*, Volumes 1 + 2. In recent years, he leads bridge and sightseeing groups to other countries, found on his travel website: baronbridgetravel.com.

For more information on Randy Baron's *Blue Ribbon Conventions* series, please visit **www.BaronBarclay.com**

BARON BARCLAY BRIDGE SUPPLY
Practice. Play. Teach.

$8.95
ISBN 978-1-944201-35-7
50895>
9 781944 201357

www.baronbarclay.com

ONE NOTRUMP FORCING AUCTIONS (CONTINUED)

4 An invitational hand with a long suit. For example:

OPENER	RESPONDER
1♠	1NT (forcing)
2♦	3♥

5 A hand that is not quite strong enough to insist on game.

6 Exploring for a partscore with no fit for partner.

RESPONDING TO 1NT FORCING

Because responder may be looking to bid his suit and escape without the auction getting too high, opener shouldn't rebid his suit without six. The first option for opener without a six-card suit is to bid a four-card suit on the second round (with 4-5-2-2 distribution, you have a dilemma, because you probably don't want to bid 2♠, forcing your partner to bid on the three-level. Some partnerships make this the only exception to rebidding a five-card suit; others bid 2♠ or a two-card minor. This is a good auction to discuss. Some pairs use the Flannery convention to solve this problem when you are specifically 4-5-2-2 by opening 2D with 11-15 HCP and this distribution). He may be forced to bid a three-card minor without six of his opening suit or a four-card suit. The following box shows the possible rebids after a 1NT response:

With a minimum opening bid:

1. Rebid a six-card or longer suit.
2. Bid a lower-ranking four or five card suit.
3. Bid a three-card minor. (Some players use a 2♦ rebid to show a four-card suit, so 2♣ only promises two).

With more than a minimum opening bid:

4. Jump in a six-card or longer suit.
5. Raise to 2NT, or with a good enough hand, jump to 3NT.
6. Make a jump shift.
7. Reverse to 2♠ after opening 1♥.
8. Make a bid at the two level if 4-7 aren't good alternatives, and show extra strength later in the auction if you have a chance.

IS ONE NOTRUMP FORCING BY A PASSED HAND?

Many experts disagree on the answer; there are valid reasons to play it forcing, semi-forcing, or non-forcing over a major suit opening, depending on your system and preference. In recent years, the tendency has been toward playing it non-forcing, but your partnership can decide this. One understanding you might have: If you have a full opening bid, you can play it as forcing; if you have a minimum or sub-minimum, you can pass 1NT without a convenient rebid.

WHEN THE ENEMY COMPETES OVER 1NT FORCING

If RHO bids or doubles partner's 1NT Forcing response to your opening bid, this relieves you of any obligation to bid. Depending on your hand, this can be either a blessing or a curse. There is never any reason to bid a three-card suit; if you make a bid in this situation, it's because you want to describe your hand further, not because you had to do this. All rebids keep their same meaning as when the opponent didn't bid. Here are a few examples:

OPENER (YOU)	LHO	RESPONDER (PARTNER)	RHO
1♠	Pass	1NT (Forcing)	2♣

1
♠ A K 7 4 2
♥ Q 9 3
♦ A 10 9 2
♣ 4

Bid 2♦, the same call you would have made without the 2♣ call.

2
♠ A 10 8 7 5
♥ K Q 6
♦ K 8 7
♣ 6 3

Pass. Although you would have had to bid 2♦ if RHO had passed, you don't have to bid.

3
♠ K Q J 8 3
♥ K Q J
♦ 10 8 7
♣ A Q

2NT. Make the same call you would have taken if RHO had passed. You shouldn't double with only two clubs; with better clubs, you could consider doubling.

Here are a few quizzes to test your knowledge of 1NT Forcing auctions:

OPENER (YOU)	LHO	RESPONDER (PARTNER)	RHO
1♥	Pass	1NT	Pass
?			

1
♠ K 7 3
♥ A J 10 7 2
♦ A 7 3
♣ J 9

2♦. You cannot rebid your hearts and you are bidding your better minor. If you are playing that 2♦ shows at least 4 in the suit, you will have to bid your two-card club suit on this hand.

2
♠ 9 7 2
♥ K Q J 8 5 4
♦ K 7
♣ A 3

2♥. 6 or more hearts and a minimum.

3
♠ --
♥ A K Q 7 5
♦ A K J 10 4
♣ Q 4 2

3♦. A jump shift which is forcing to game.

OPENER (YOU)	LHO	RESPONDER (PARTNER)	RHO
1♠	Pass	1NT	Pass
2♦	Pass	?	

1
♠ 7
♥ K J 8 7 4 2
♦ J 5
♣ K 10 6 5

2♥. Natural and non-forcing.

2
♠ 9
♥ K 10 7 5
♦ Q J 10 6 2
♣ A J 8

3♦. Invitational.

3
♠ J 5
♥ A 7 5 4
♦ Q 8 7
♣ J 6 5 4

2♠. This hand is showing a false preference since your 5-2 fit is probably your best place to play.

4
♠ 8
♥ Q 9 6
♦ J 9 7 3
♣ A K J 8 3

2NT. Invitational.

SOME USEFUL CONVENTIONS TO PLAY WITH TWO OVER ONE

- Bergen raises
- Cue bidding for slam exploration
- Fourth Suit Forcing
- Help-suit game try (or some type of game try)
- Jacoby 2NT
- Keycard or Roman Keycard Blackwood (3014 or 1430)
- Negative Doubles
- New Minor Forcing
- Reverses
- Splinter bids

Please note that you can play Two Over One Game Force with the Precision Club and other forcing club systems; they fit together easily.

PUBLICATIONS TO HELP YOU LEARN TWO OVER ONE

- Bergen- Improve your 2/1 Game Force Bidding
- Bruno & Hardy- Two Over One: An Introduction
- Cohen- Larry Cohen Teaches 2/1
- Grant & Rodwell- Two Over One Game Force
- Hardy- Two Over One Game Force
- Lawrence- Workbook on the 2 over 1 System
- Seagram- 2/1 Cheat Sheet
- Thurston- 25 Steps to Learning 2/1

BARON BARCLAY

BLUE RIBBON CONVENTIONS

BY Randy Baron

TWO OVER ONE GAME FORCE

The passing years bring progress and innovation in every aspect of our lives. Bridge is no exception. Although the play of the hand by experts and good players was already at a very high level 25 or 50 years ago, the same cannot be said for bidding methods. Auctions in those "old days" were primitive compared with what today's players use. Now many club and tournament players have adopted sophisticated systems, and they can bid more accurately than most experts in the past.

T0123970
www.bar

HISTORY

Two Over One Game Force is simpler, more accurate than Standard American, and relatively easy to learn. Just like with Standard American and other bidding systems, there are countless agreements you can play, so it is helpful to have a regular partner. You can discuss your bidding methods and fill out your convention card, so that you both are comfortable with what you are playing. No matter what level player you are, you probably will find Two Over One helps you reach better contracts without too much study or changing much of what you are already comfortable with, because it is a very natural and logical system.

In the early days of its development, Two Over One was sometimes called Walsh, because it originated in the 1960s by Richard Walsh, Paul Soloway and John Swanson. Max Hardy and other experts developed it further in the decades after that.

THE DEFINITION OF TWO OVER ONE GAME FORCE

Two Over One is a bidding system that is similar to Standard American. Its most important principle: When responder bids a lower-ranking suit at the two level, after partner's opening bid at the one level, the partnership is committed to reach at least a game contract.

There are exactly SIX auctions that are Two Over One:

1♦ 2♣ - 1♥ 2♣ - 1♥ 2♦ - 1♠ 2♣ - 1♠ 2♦ - 1♠ 2♥

In these six examples, the opponents have passed between the opening bid and the response. It is important to note that there are various ways to play Standard American, just as there are many variations of Standard American. As I discuss the system, I will give you my recommendations; other authors and partners use different agreements.

Most players have decided that in the auction:

NORTH (YOU)	EAST (OPPONENT)	SOUTH (PARTNER)
1♠	2♣	2♦ or 2♥

when the opponents have entered the bidding and your partner bids a new suit at the two level, it is still forcing to game. In this situation, partner has other bids available if he doesn't have a good enough hand to insist that you reach game.

Note that auctions such as 1♦/2♠ or 1♠/2♥ are NOT Two Over One. These bids at the two level are higher-ranking than the opening bid, so they have a different meaning (usually a very weak, intermediate or very strong hand is being shown by the responder, depending on the partnership agreement).

WHY SHOULD I PLAY TWO OVER ONE?

Because the system is NATURAL and LOGICAL, Two Over One allows you and your partner to describe your distribution and limit your strength more easily than with Standard bidding. When the auction proceeds 1♥/2♣, neither of you has to worry about whether the next bids are forcing or non-forcing, because you must keep bidding until you at least reach game. In many sequences, the partnership has a better idea early in the auction how high you should bid; there is more guesswork in most Standard auctions. With Two Over One, you usually can take your time to bid more slowly and more scientifically than with Standard, so you can confidently arrive at the best contract. It allows you to explore for slam more easily by often establishing a forcing sequence that isn't available in Standard. It's usually unnecessary to jump when you or your partner has a strong hand, taking up valuable bidding space as you attempt to find the best contract.

A helpful feature of Two Over One (as with Standard and other systems) is that you can add virtually any conventions. As with Standard, it's a good idea to proceed slowly when you make changes to your card; make sure your partnership is completely comfortable with a convention before adding others.

WHAT ARE THE DISADVANTAGES?

As an advocate for Two Over One, I don't acknowledge that there are many problems you will encounter in learning the system. Even inexperienced players frequently make a very easy time learning and understanding it. The main weakness of Two Over One is One Notrump Forcing, which is often necessary. Although many auctions after a Forcing Notrump work out fine, they can lead to inaccurate or awkward sequences. Whenever our partnership has a Forcing Notrump bid, I hope that we will land in a reasonable final contract. We might play a 4-3 or 5-2 fit, which isn't the end of the world, or miss the best contract. The good news is that most of the field will have similar issues, because One Notrump Forcing is almost mandatory when playing Five Card Majors (whether Standard or Two Over One).

QUIZ ON TWO OVER ONE AUCTIONS

Which of the following auctions are forcing to game playing Two Over One?

1

NORTH	EAST	SOUTH
1♥	Pass	2♣

2

NORTH	EAST	SOUTH
1♣	Pass	2♥

3

NORTH	EAST	SOUTH
1♦	Pass	2♣

4

NORTH	EAST	SOUTH
1♦	2♣	2♥

5

NORTH	EAST	SOUTH
1♠	Pass	2♠

6

NORTH	EAST	SOUTH
1♠	Double	2♣

7

NORTH	EAST	SOUTH
1♠	1NT	2♥

8

NORTH	EAST	SOUTH
1♥	2♣	2♦

Your partner opens 1♥ and the RHO passes. On which of these hands should you force to game?

9

♠ K75
♥ A J
♦ K J
♣ Q 10 8 7 5 2

10

♠ K Q 8 3
♥ Q 7 6
♦ Q 6 3
♣ A J 7

11

♠ A Q 7
♥ J 10 9 4
♦ 9
♣ A 8 7 4 2

12

♠ J 5 2
♥ Q
♦ Q J 10 8 6 3
♣ A 8 4

QUIZ ANSWERS

Which of the following auctions are forcing to game playing Two Over One?

1 Yes.

2 No. This is not a Two Over One bid. It's a jump shift which can be weak, intermediate or strong, depending on your partnership agreement.

3 Yes.

4 Yes, even though there has been interference (some partners play this as forcing for one round, not forcing to game).

5 No. This is a simple raise, and not a new suit.

6 No. Over the takeout double, this is not Two Over One.

7 No. Over a 1NT overcall by the opponent, a new suit isn't forcing; with a good hand, you would probably double.

8 Yes, even though there has been interference (see #4).

---

9 Yes, you have enough to force to game by bidding 2♣.

10 Yes, although you shouldn't bid 2♣ or 2♦. The correct bid is 1♠ by bidding your 4-card major, and you will make sure your partnership reaches game.

11 Yes. Although you only have 11 HCP, you should make sure you reach game. If you play Splinter bids, you should bid 4♦.

12 No. You don't have enough strength to force to game. As we'll discuss, you should bid 1NT Forcing.

HOW MANY POINTS ARE REQUIRED TO OPEN THE BIDDING AND FORCE TO GAME AS RESPONDER?

Playing Two Over One, you should open the same hands as you would open playing Standard (from 11-13 HCP, depending on your rules and style). To force to game after partner opens the bidding on the one level, you should have 12 or 13 points opposite a solid opening bid to insist on game. If you have a fit with partner, you should add distributional points to the high card points.

RAISING PARTNER'S 1♥ OR 1♠ OPENING BID

Whenever you have found an eight-card or longer fit in a major suit, you should strive to play in that suit. So here are some rules that you should follow (similar to Standard):

1. With 6-9 points (always include distribution points once you have found a fit) and 3-card support for partner's suit, raise partner to the 2-level (1♥ / 2♥ or 1♠ / 2♠).
2. With 7-9 points and 4-card support for partner's suit, bid 3♣ (1♥ / 3♣ or 1♠ / 3♣). This is a Bergen raise.
3. With 10-12 points and 4-card support for partner's suit, bid 3♦ (1♥ /3♦ or 1♠ / 3♦). This is also a Bergen raise.
4. With 13+ points and at least 4-card support for opener's major suit, you should make a Splinter Bid (with a singleton or a void) or make a forcing raise such as Jacoby 2NT.
5. With 2-6 points and 4-card support for opener's major, you should make a preemptive raise (1♥ / 3♥ or 1♠ / 3♠).
6. With 10-12 points and 3-card support for opener's major, you should make a Forcing One Notrump response, which I will discuss in the next pages.

The methods I have suggested above are among the most popular currently. There are various other ways to show support when your side has opened 1♥ or 1♠. One of the recommended Two Over One books will show you options.

ONE NOTRUMP FORCING AUCTIONS

As I said above, 1NT Forcing doesn't always lead to a perfect result. It is crucial to understand this bid well when playing Two Over One (or Standard American). It is a versatile tool, allowing your partnership to describe various types of hands, which would be more of a problem without 1NT Forcing.

One Notrump Forcing can be used effectively when you have:

1. 10-12 points and 3-card support (a limit raise). For example:

OPENER	RESPONDER
1♠	1NT (forcing)
2♣	3♠

2. An invitational, balanced hand (about good 10 to a bad 12 points, and no fit for partner's suit). For example:

OPENER	RESPONDER
1♥	1NT (forcing)
2♦	2NT

3. A weak hand with a long suit (it's difficult to show this hand in any other way). For example:

OPENER	RESPONDER
1♠	1NT (forcing)
2♣	2♥

Continue on other side